My First Book About Bees

Amazing Animal Books
Children's Picture Books

By Molly Davidson

Mendon Cottage Books

JD-Biz Publishing

Read More Amazing Animal Books

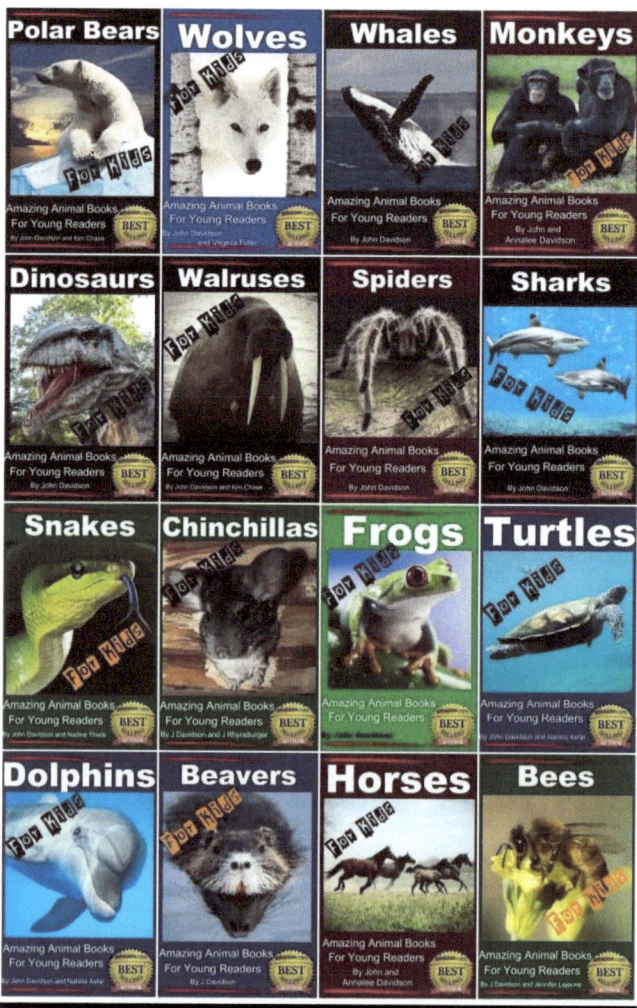

Purchase at Amazon.com

Table of Contents

What Are Bees? 4

Facts About Bees 6

Options for treating bee stings.................................9

The Life Cycle of a Bee..11

Why Are Bees So Important to Humans? 13

Types of Bees...14

Carpenter bees...14

Africanized honey bees...15

Bumble Bees 17

Yellow Jackets 18

Wasps..19

The Bee Hive 20

The Honey Bee Colony 23

The Royal Queen 26

Bee Keeping..28

Tips for Preventing Attacks 30

Harvesting Honey 35

Honey..36

What is Pollen and Pollination?..............................38

Flowers That Attract Bees 40

Conclusion 42

Publisher 49

What Are Bees?

Bees are related to ants and wasps.

Bees are made up of three body parts, the head, thorax, and abdomen.

The thorax is the smaller middle section of the body containing three pair of legs and four wings.

Bees' wings flap 11,400 times per minute, that is why we hear a buzzing sound.

The abdomen is the lower and largest part of the body that has a nectar pouch and stomach, at the end is the stinger.

Facts About Bees

1. A honey bee is not born knowing how to make honey, they are taught by more experienced bees.

2. A honey bee will make only 1/12 of a teaspoon of honey in its lifetime.

3. Bees have been around 30 million years.

4. Bees are cold blooded.

5. Bees communicate through smells and dances.

6. Bees can fly up to 15 miles per hour.

7. A hive will fly almost 100,000 miles to collect
   2.2 pounds of honey.

Options for treating bee stings

After a sting the first step is always to remove the stinger and wash the site.

Here are a few methods to do next (pick one):

1. Apply ice for 20 minutes.

2. Apply toothpaste for 15 minutes.

3. Make a paste out of baking soda, vinegar and meat tenderizer, apply for 20 minutes.

4. Apply calamine lotion

5. Apply hydrocortisone cream.

6. Apply honey for 30 minutes.

Remember, that bees do us more good than they do harm and are a beautiful part of nature that we get to enjoy in more ways than one!

The Life Cycle of a Bee

There are four different stages of a bees' life cycle.

Stage 1: The queen lays soft white eggs, the egg stays an egg for 3 days.

Stage 2: On the third day, it's a pupa. It now has eyes, wings, and legs.

Stage 3: The bee will chew its way out of the cell. It becomes an adult on day 16.

Stage 4: Work! Bees will clean, feed larvae, produce wax, guard the hive, and gather nectar to make honey.

Worker bees live for about 45 days.

Why Are Bees So Important to Humans?

Bees do 80% of the pollination, which is what makes plants grow.

One bee hive will visit more than 2 million flowers per year, gathering 66 pounds of pollen!

Types of Bees

Carpenter bees

Carpenter bees are large bees found throughout the world.

These bees build their nests inside wood.

Carpenter bees usually by themselves or girls may live with a small group of other girls.

Africanized honey bees

Africanized bees are known as "killer bees."

They will attack animals or humans who come into their area.

They like to live by the water, and will swamp when it is about to rain.

These bees were brought from Africa to Brazil, and

have migrated north, to some states in the U.S.

They are mostly found in California, Texas, Arizona, and New Mexico.

Bumble Bees

Bumble bees are yellow and black furry bees that spend most of their time pollinating plants.

Bumble bees do not build hives, they just find somewhere soft to nest, like in leaves.

Yellow Jackets

Yellow jackets like sweet things, like your lemonade or ice cream.

So be careful on a hot summer day, the yellow jackets will find your sweet treat.

They make a paper like substance by chewing wood; this is what they make their nests out of.

Wasps

Wasps are very helpful to farmers, they eat pest insects that try and eat crops.

Wasps are skinner than other bees, and can be bright yellow, red, and even brown.

Wasps can be very mean, leave them alone, they will sting over and over again.

The Bee Hive

A bee hive is the house or nest that the bees make to live in.

When a colony of bees needs a new home, they send out "scout" bees who will fly as far as 55 miles to find a new location.

Bees will carry honey with them to their new hive which they chew up to make beeswax, this will hold the new honey.

Hives have an entrance at the bottom which will have some guard bees watching it.

The bees squeeze into the hive to keep it really

warm, about 90°F.

Healthy hives can have up to 80,000 bees!

The Honey Bee Colony

There are three different types of bees that live inside a colony.

1. **The queen bee:** There is only one queen; she is the only bee to lay eggs. The queen can live from 3-5 years, which is longer than any other bee!

2. Worker bees: there are anywhere from 30,000 to 70,000 worker bees in a colony.

They are all girls, they do all the work. They clean, feed the queen, gather pollen, and fan new air into the hive by flapping their wings.

Worker bees have a stinger but die soon after they have stung.

3. Drones: Drones are the boy bees, they do not have stingers.

They only help in getting the queen pregnant, so she can lay eggs.

The queen does not lay eggs during the winter, so in the fall all the drones are pushed out of the hive; they don't need them until spring.

The Royal Queen

The queen is picked when she is still an egg.

She is fed "royal jelly" which makes her be able to lay eggs.

She lays 2,000 - 3,000 eggs per day.

She releases a smell that tells the whole hive how to act and what to do.

She is so busy a worker bee does everything for her. They clean her, feed her, and remove her waste (so she doesn't have to leave the hive to go to the bathroom).

Bee Keeping

First you will need hive boxes. You can buy them or make them, but they need to be bright colors.

Next, you will need to add bees, you can buy worker bees and have them delivered by mail.

The best time to start beekeeping is at the end of spring.

You need about 12,000 bees and one queen, to get started.

You will need to check on your bees, while wearing a bee suit, to see that they are producing honey, the queen is laying eggs, and to check for disease.

When working with your bees, you need to stay calm, so they will stay calm too.

Tips for Preventing Attacks

Tips for preventing attacks:

1. Check around your house and trees for bee colonies.

2. Do not try to remove bee hives without professional help.

3. Keep pets and kids inside while doing yard work, which can make bees angry.

4. Cover your chimney when not in use.

5. Notice when you see a few bees to see if there is a colony nearby.

6. Have an escape plan.

7. Wear light colored clothing.

8. Do not wear perfume while doing yard work.

When an attack happens:

1. Quickly get into a house or car and close all doors and windows.

2. Do not jump in a pool, the bees will wait until you come up to attack.

3. Run away very quickly, do not stop.

4. Protect your face, because bee stings on the face and head are much more dangerous than those on the body, cover your head with your shirt if that is your only thing you have.

Harvesting Honey

It is easiest to leave the honey comb, and just take the honey.

You can buy an electric honey extractor, but they are expensive.

You can take the honey comb too; it is used for candles, soaps, and lotions.

Honey

You can sell your honey.

Honey is a very nutritious food containing, trace enzymes, minerals, vitamins, and amino acids!

The color of honey depends on what flowers the nectar was taken from.

There are more than 300 different kinds of honey.

What is Pollen and Pollination?

Pollination leads to the creation of new seeds that grow into new plants.

Boy plants make pollen, the girl plants catch it with their sticky pistil, the inside of the flower top.

Flowers cannot move to make this happen, so insects, animals, and the wind help them do this.

When bees, flies, butterflies, or birds come to get nectar from a plant, the pollen sticks to them.

Then, when they fly to the next plant, the pollen falls off, now this plant is pollinated.

Plants that are pollinated by insects are usually bright colored to catch the insects' attention.

Flowers That Attract Bees

If you want to grow a beautiful garden, you will need the help of bees for pollination.

The best thing to do is go to your local nursery; start

with native plants, the bees will be use to them.

Bees also like herbs, like thyme, mint, and basil.

Flower colors that bees love are blue, purple, white, and yellow.

Bees like sweet fruit and vegetables too.

Some of their favorites are berries, cantaloupe, cucumbers, squash, pumpkins, peppers, and watermelon.

Conclusion

Bees are amazing little insects and without them our World would not be as wonderful.

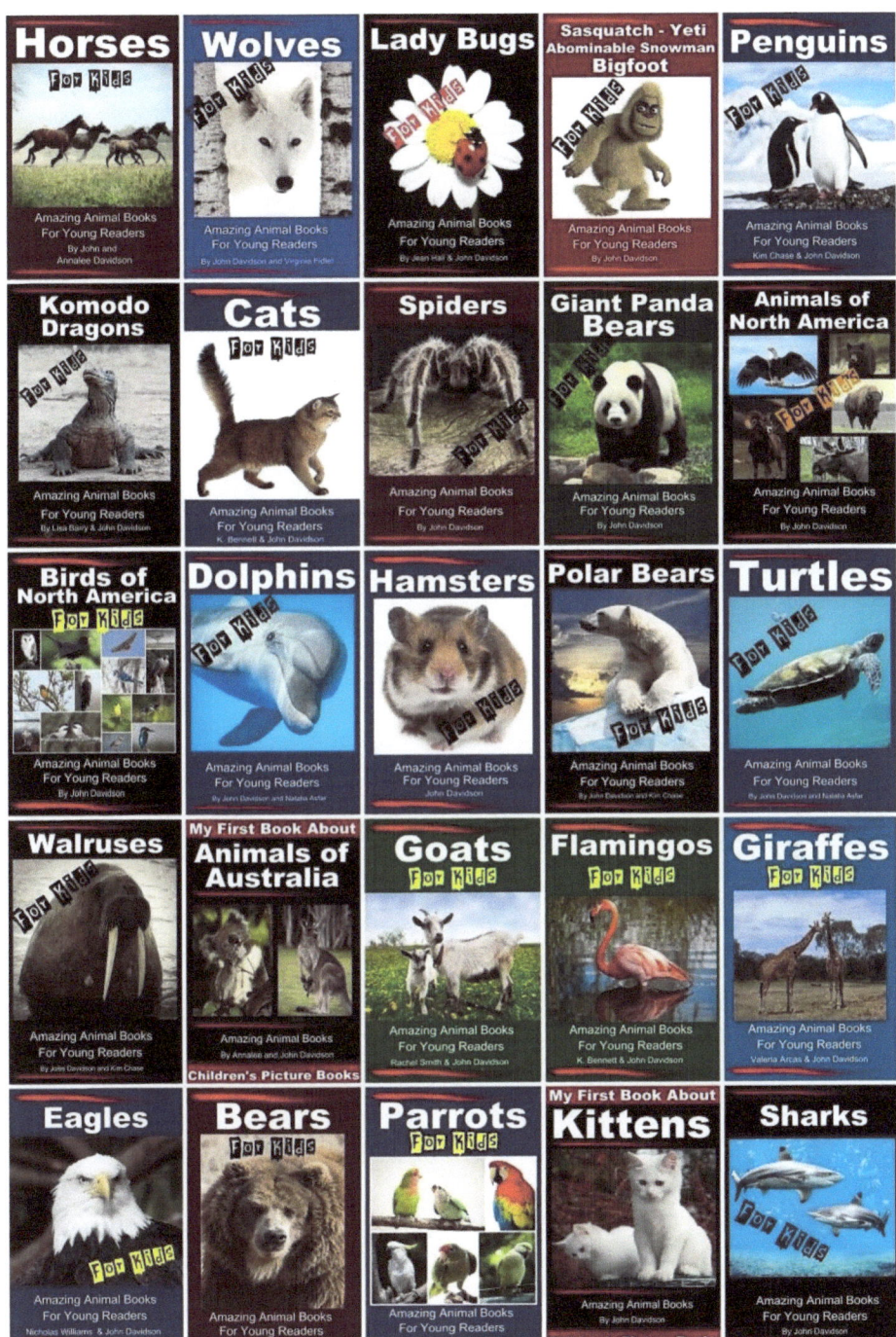

Our books are available at

1. Amazon.com

2. Barnes and Noble

3. Itunes

4. Kobo

5. Smashwords

6. Google Play Books

Download Free Books!
http://MendonCottageBooks.com

Publisher

JD-Biz Corp

P O Box 374

Mendon, Utah 84325

http://www.jd-biz.com/

Mendon Cottage Books

P O Box 374, Mendon Utah 84325